Strike

Rebecca Dunham

New Issues Poetry & Prose

A Green Rose Book

New Issues Poetry & Prose
The College of Arts and Sciences
Western Michigan University
Kalamazoo, Michigan 49008

First Edition, 2019.

ISBN: 978-1-936970-60-5 (paperbound)

Library of Congress Cataloging-in-Publication Data:
Dunham, Rebecca
Strike/Rebecca Dunham
Library of Congress Control Number: 2018947277

Editor:	William Olsen
Managing Editor:	Kimberly Kolbe
Layout Editor:	Danielle Isaiah
Assistant Editors:	Andrew Collard, Alyssa Jewell,
	Sara Lupita Olivares
Art Direction:	Nicholas Kuder
Design:	Brandon Smith
Production:	Paul Sizer
	The Design Center, Frostic School of Art
	College of Fine Arts
	Western Michigan University
Printing:	McNaughton & Gunn, Inc.

Strike

Rebecca Dunham

New Issues

WESTERN MICHIGAN UNIVERSITY

Also by Rebecca Dunham

The Miniature Room
The Flight Cage
Glass Armonica
Cold Pastoral

Contents

V. The Year I Turned Old

White Flag

Once I vowed
I would forgive him anything.
But it's not a matter of will.
This earth, a brittle North.
This day, how it drops me
to my knees. Impossible
that the half-gone grass,
matted with frost, feels
the same to him as to me,
that this sky flows an identical
alloy of steel. Strike
the match. Torch the dead
heap of leaves before me.
A black forecast stings my eyes.
How can I forgive
when I can't even stand,
when I can't even find
the earth beneath my feet? When
I keel, hope-choked, and
it's not that I don't want to.
It's that I can't.

I.

Mrs.

Whetstone

After the former custom of hanging
a whetstone round the neck of a liar.

This house burnt numb. Someone
should rub it warm if I will
not. I will not. Do I remember?
the drowning man asks. The once-us?
his fish-mouth begs. I
do. Scotch in the garage, I say,
wine cabineted, secrets, and even
his prone body, dead man's float in
the TV's rash of light. Another
cotton-night. The clock keeps time.

::

Life like a frieze, and there
is no sound. Like a heart
on screen, pure mute, I grow
beautiful: carved cold.
My children mouth words. They
speak in black and white. I let
the lake take him, their
father, his arms like two wings.
I watch him sink down.

::

I am that hard. I do
not extend my hand, do not
stop him. The raft moves
in waves. I watch. I am stone.

::

I will mineral my ears—will
not curl in upon myself, but think

in sculpted relief. I want
to step free, clear, to touch
my children's brows like the sky's
winterblue. To cool with.
To take my two children in my two
snow-perfect marble arms.

Anger, According to Mrs.

As if anger could be a kind of vocation for some women. It is a chilly thought. —Anne Carson

Before, anger was copper wire, sparked,
a furious halo of heat and electricity, everything laid to waste

—ponds boiled, the charred trout, trees and grass blacked out—

Before, my anger was an acetylene torch.

Before, I was a girl and anger was a tantrum
and I was brushfire gorging myself and
it was the blooded palm applied to both my cheeks.

Before, like a spire, the direction of anger burned up.

      Now I could hit this note
      a thousand times and still it
      wouldn't be enough. It is never
      enough. Now,

anger doesn't catch and flower, but presses
      down and in, cold density
of platinum on skin.

Now anger is armor, is two smelted plates
harnessed to my frame.

Now ice burns quite as well as any matchbook flame.

Now anger splits field and sky like a sea of spade-black ships

      and this anger never forgets.

The Wedding Processional, as Sung by Mrs.

"Raise, boys, your torches! Raise them high!
I see the scarf of crimson nigh." —Catullus

Now will come the bride, Vesta's temple swept clean.
Six ribboned locks of hair hidden by her red-
orange veil, its flame the mate of his own. *Oh*
Hymen, come hither—

The mother slips her own mother's purse into
her daughter's hand, just as she's stripped away: wool,
alum and cedar gum. Stash of lead with its
vial of oil.

Do not speak it. A secret: she has only
to stray to find her exile, island of rock—
salted foam and crash of freedom—if only
she can forget his

fingers unknotting the bridal belt. Forget
the honeyed taste of her new name on his lips.
Come forth and hear the hymn we pour out for thee—
hear the cord fall loose.

Bring forth the bride, the fire—distaff and twine—
and Lucretia's poignard blade: Fidelity
demands not only virtue's deep mortal stab,
but the love of it.

The Wedding at Cana

The first sign—
how her husband could tilt

the earthen jug
and the wine would flow red
        as a liar's tongue.

      ::

There is always enough
—the bottle need never empty—
A blind man, he bends to
the closet's dark recess, reaching.

Faith is strict, insists on its blood
sacrifice—the liver, the heart,
the organ plying its warm, ruddy
tones—the ever-swelling hymn.

This is how one makes water
into wine—

      ::

Discards chime in the recycling bin.
She listens to the wind.

Rain of emptied glass, its pour,
when she opens the attic scuttle door.

At the liquor store, the clerk can
greet her three-year-old girl by name.

      ::

The first miracle—
        Veronese gives us Christ,
expressionless, a man
in a stupor. The wedding guests
frown, eyes lost—mourning—

Above Christ, a man butchers
                    the lamb, cleaver
stilled in the second before
its descent. Always

he must suffer this. The drawn knife
always just above his head.

Incarnadine

"*The Tulip Era*"
Sultan Ahmed III, Constantinople

And his hunger an open
wound whose broken edges he cannot
bind closed, not

      by cut blossoms
      in their glass bottles, not by

mirrored illusion—

      each over-flexed petal tied
      by hand to a point needle-fine

paper-sleeved bulbs
banked and bedded, a harem:

      each pollen-heavy anther
      worth its millioned weight in gold

each tulip candle-lit
and labeled in silver filigree—night

      after night, this mania takes him,
      cell by cell,

leaving him only
sharp stitch of daggered color

The Visitation

She tries to bring herself to care.
        Him, him—it is always about him.
Some days she wants to dress
        all in white. Some days she wants

to flood her body cobalt and iridium,
        wants to glow from the inside out.
Wants to walk the rehabilitation ward's
        halls and touch each penitent's bowed

head. His she will not. It is not her
        he shakes for. Sweat on his temple.
Eyes down. And something akin
        to caring splinters her haze, at last. Yes,

she likes to see him here, like this.

Gaslighting

I don't know what you're talking about,
he says. Choke-

damp, fire-damp, this mine
shaft's spirits thicket me, lies

chambered and *you're the one who—*

Over the butcher
paper's sheets, my red story sprawls.

His love is a will-o'-the-wisp,
is moon-lantern, the only way through
marsh and bog.

Doubts teeter, a scarlet fever and lunge—

This is the ritual.

How he can make color disappear.
How he can step-

ladder into my skull and decline
what he finds.

In one light, a vermeil trail of falsehood

and tarnish. In another: stainless
steel sink, clink of silver in the drawer

and denial
beaten to silver foil, to silver leaf.

The Kept

Secrets require silence and my lips
stake an impassable weight.

Cast in lost-wax, my body makes and remakes itself
each night. A spruing-webbed bestiary—

> Bats hung amid snaking bronze boughs.
> The man with a nose like a rhino's horn.
> Her death mask plastered, at the ready.

—A woman, granite-feathered and scaled.

I run my fingers along her single wing.
I knew her even before I knew her.

> In sickness and in sorrow,
our eyes like four blue vaults.

Forgiveness

I sit in the buckthorn's shade.
It does not belong here
any more than me, invasive
and spitting forth its many-limbed
progeny, a nest of angry snakes.
It must be purged, cut back
       and stump-ground.
There will be no rising
from this grave. How do we learn
to let go? Wind-shivered,
the bush shakes its green-tinctured
leaves, its garlands of poison fruit.

As if to say the flesh does not know.
As if the answer will always be no.

II.

A Narrative of the Captivity and Restoration of Mrs.

Sanctuary, said the house, but it wasn't—

If tempted to go home

The first betrayal
is the betrayal of one's self
and that gate's lock
cannot be picked.
Heap of tortured hairpins
at my feet. I admit
the apothecary's cordial,
its gentian whorling
my parted lips livid as
the drowned. A cold caution.
A single flame blue
burning in a leadplant.
Love: not for a moment
can I believe. Why subtract
myself when so many
hunger to do it for me?
What comfort could I
turn to? At this place
we continued many days.

Black creatures in the night

You tabulate our attributes.
But the wolf lives in a blank
of reed-fringed exile. I am
her bark as it pounds forth its
arrows, its battle tumult,
its echolalia of apology
and bargaining and blame.
The wolf wears her insides
on the outside: *Woman is that
creature.* I want to live in
No-Man's Land. I want to raze
the moon. Husband, I vow
the wolf curves: mercuric, raw,
ever-moving. You have felt her
snarl close in bed. You
are the one to twine your legs
around the wilderness she has
staked beneath our sheets.

The house on fire over our heads

And yet we shiver—
below its roof a glitter
like frost webs
our skin, carpets tacked
over window and door.
Unflared, the heart-
blood mats, flat
as flax and hemp beneath
my heels. My tears like
hail. My fever a burnt
ice. I never fail to marvel
how our bodies
give way to the sofa's
frayed cushions, how
we go on breathing
this smoke that chokes us
cold.

Morning, I must turn my back upon

The front door pens me
in, my husband off
to work. Stiff-
tongued, the wound
sickens. I could sink
under this affliction, this
little fire that blisters
beneath my skin. He
departs, the plates left
for me to clean, I am
always cleaning up
his messes: not hungover
but overtired, not cruel but
honest, he says. Throw
a snow-husked bough on
the day. To thaw last
night's bitter freeze—
snow-squall blown in
as predicted—my lips lit
blue as a match's flame.
I must bear it.
The angry heat that follows.

This was the comfort I had

One. Tree branches like black
rivers veining the sky, oak
leaves left to scab our yard.
Two. What he likes to say, each night:

You think you're—. And, *There's
a reason*. I know it has
passed when (*three*) I don't even
bother. How do you bury a mirage?

Four. I pull up the sheets.
He watches Mad Men on TV. Scotch,
neat. Rings on the table.
And it is all the same to me.

III.

The Impossible Bed

Three Soliloquies, as Performed by Mrs.

1. Lou Andreas-Salomé

It is not me but curiosity
        that kills in the sea's green
field: its victims like the sirens'
heap of bones, flesh still

half-bound by them—
           the heart's
blood trails up, unwinding
like a long, red snake:

rapacious, unrelenting, all
tracks may lead to me but none
come back out—

2. *Mrs. Pontellier*

He would clip a cockatoo's wings,
that man who calls me *Mine*.
A feather-white dress, my wifely
act, never enough to sate

him. It was over before
it began. Thrashed beneath
the waves, there's no more reason
for me to lie—I didn't

need a sea to drown. To awaken
fury's black-beaked hook was
all it took to tear my lungs and drop me,
bruise-lipped, to battered shore.

3. *Mary Ann Simpson as Matty Tyler*

I hiss, boiling, my touch saltpeter and steam,
vanadium, incendiary as a god in heat.
Mouth to my skin, he dares taste, dares try to
       devour me whole.

Each time we fuck, his starched sheets turn black
beneath me. Soot in a fire. And my silk
dress smokes—its hot cloud my devil's breath:
       that which unties

a man's very substance from itself. That
which annuls. It is simple chemistry. I am the one
left to pick up the pieces, to arrange them
       as I see fit.

Woman in Glass

Forthwith [Zeus] made an evil thing for men as the price of fire.
—Hesiod, "The Theogeny"

Always, fire exacts its char-white price.

    Your torch: a lurid rose.
    Your touch: of molded earth.

And me: I will be
the dirt thrown on men's red fevers.

That which sticks in the maw of hell.

My only failure the failure to conceive
what man is capable of—

In the mirror, the glass girl's mouth
cracked open as a snake's

    by your hands, your forceps'
    double-spooned grip.

They clamp and stretch her tongue.

Beneath: a single sphere, pearled silver.
You never listen.

    Just because you can do a thing
    doesn't mean you should.

The Interlocutor

I know many men, many
of whom say they practice
kindness to all

Men. To them, they say,
Man is just a synonym for *Human,*
nothing but a noun

one can put in its place.
They tell me to
put myself at ease. To drift

safe in grammar's amniotic
embrace. It is nothing
to them, the power

that a single key can strike.
Pinched with concern, their soft
brown eyes regard me.

No matter how hard
they try, they cannot see why
I care, why it might matter

that so much relies
on the difference between
men and *Men*, Shift + M.

In the Bedroom

Two-faced, he spits, as if
                        it's a bad thing.

As if the first lesson we learn
isn't to look both ways

             before we cross, as if
there aren't two sides to every story.

He slams the door
           shut. End of Subject.

He doesn't want to know

how, like a sole confessor, I
can divulge and absolve
               in turn. The way

out is all I ask for—
that threshold.
              Shameful and shame-
less, he says. Yes I am

and yes, I am that, too.

Tensile

If he can throw it, you can take it.

Spatula clatter on Formica. Plate slivers like confetti. Like when you're at a party and the lights flick on and shout and your eyes can't catch up to the bright clamor and it can take a minute—*Can I have just a minute?*—to recognize the walls the floor the coffee stain in the shape of your eternal savior's face.

You can take a slap, starfish red, red as his boot treads clogged with Virginia clay. You can sweep and bandage and dump the evidence in the bin and when he asks the next day you can smile and say *all boxed up* and he'll give you a kiss.

The ground tips and troughs in flashes. Green air spins electric. Vibrates over the stagger and hum of your stolid white fridge. You know all about last legs. You know how to measure the tension in a man's face to the precise pound per square inch, how to predict weather with a single glance and you might as well swipe that coffee stain clean. Might as well shut your ears.

You don't need anyone to tell you your fortune.

Capillary Action

She strips lashes of white linen
from their bed. Shoves

his worn sofa out the door,
into the garage. Into that newly

hollowed space. Tomorrow, she will
torque the garden hose's rusted

valve open. Like her father's heart
after his attack, it will ache. Ice-

rivers will rush the garage floor, will
wick up the sofa's red twill sides

until she feels it's safe to call it
wrecked. To push it to the curb.

Who cares what the neighbors think.
It's someone else's problem now.

IV.

Tableaux Vivants

The producing and forming of *tableaux vivants* have been
the author's study for the past ten years.

The Living Room

"Charlotte Corday," Paul Jacques Aimé Baudre, 1860

Mannequin-still, his body
stretches the sofa's narrow length.
A dying man. A bathtub.

Its water twilled rust-red.

Scrap of green throw blanketing
his feet. Her feet won't work.

She should help or leave or—

Backlit, the door's shadow is
a knife-hilt blackening

his chest. His papers, rivered
milk, spill. The map on the wall

is mere ornament, out of date:
nothing is where it used to be.

All drift and float.

Where there used to be land, only water.
Where there used to be water, no escape.

The Backyard

"Laocoön and His Sons," 25 BC

Her children and their father rake
the grass smooth. A matched
set, the children bracket him.

Witness the fury of the disinterred:

ground bees knot burred ropes
about their feet and cord their legs.

Children carry within their parents'
sins, diseased. Pain plaits each face.

Her son's eyes on his father's.

What blue venom binds these
three, what grief will time unleash?

Then the bellow that breaks
the skies just before they scatter
like woodchips beneath the ax.

The Driveway

"*The Birth of Venus*," Sandro Botticelli, 1486

And so it was that she emerged.

Single contrapposto figure caught
on the verge of stepping forth,

of becoming—

Not labor's long-troughing waves,
nor the journey of feet on shore,

   but the instant just before.

Stand of pin-oaks, flight of posies,
and a new violet coat drawn about her.

To wait is not the same as inaction.

Soon enough the wind will bend
the cattail reeds, soon enough

she will fasten herself to the light.

V.

The Year I Turned Old

Elegy Written in Neon Lights

Circus Circus, Reno, Nevada

A single cart trundles the hotel's
long hall. Its loose wheel rattles

and soothes me like the clatter
of the train that once punctured

my childhood sleep. Its iron rails
less than a block away. No

death, no grief, no too-thin walls.
Only the gravel river of my parents'

voices to deny, the flash-flood
levels rising up the stairs after

lights out. Here, the lights never
go out. Not even when a stick-figure

body—five simple strokes
and a circle for a head—dives down

night's black page. An ink blot.
A migraine aura. Blue-green-

red—always too much red—it spins
and blinks so fast that no one

could blame anyone for missing it.

In Retrograde

Once, a girl loved a man,
all split-open skin and plattered organ.

In hell they have color and so
she donned silk blue
plumes, her breasts a nauseous green
under the madder lake sky.

Centuries abandoned
to his fragile heart, to its orbit.

What I'd have given back then to see.

::

Frozen, the hard earth steams.
The warm front presses and holds.
Hot iron on a dun cotton shirt.

A wash of gray rolls over
the highway's taut skin and dulls
all the edges.

::

Hell is other people, the famous man
once wrote. I know he thought
it was true.   But I
am spent. No kindness left
for a man so rich in others
he could mistake paradise for
a life alone.

::

I once knew a girl—not well—who
declared she wanted to be broken
by loss. She said it
out loud: *I want to be broken.*

I didn't know what to say. I said,
then you've never been broken before.
We never spoke again.
It's been twenty years. Did she

— the interstate runs barren at night—

did she welcome the blow when it came.

Mrs.: A Lexicon

> *...valuable not in themselves but as signs of other things*
> —Italo Calvino

Desire

:: a storm-chopped
pasture and I am shipwrecked beneath
its silver-fogged lake. Floor of silt, stub-spindled.
I want to lie back on it. To float on
its bed of nails.

To Forgive

:: requires first an object
to blame. A paradox. i.e., I forgive Man X for
that spiked bed (plot of red pain that grids my spine).
Forgive that (white dress frost flower) but only if
love is a white flag.

Sunday

:: is a man with a new heart,
triple-grief bypass. Is the throb of warm tap-
water over hands blued white. Is a dropped call. Is
me, wholly unaware. Then
the paramedics, like wolves at the door.

The Soul

:: a dead warehouse
switch-flick-lit by rows of fluorescent tubes
that snap and spark in turn. *One at a time,*
the shift manager says. He sees over
us all, hollows us out.

Fragments for My Father

All language is from Edgar Allen Poe's
"The Masque of the Red Death"

1. *The body as palace,*

as castellated abbey: strong and lofty
the wall that girdles it. Within

the iron gates beats feverishly
the heart of life, bolts
welded by furnace and massy hammer.

Let the world take care of itself,
he thinks. As if security lies within.

2. *His many-chambered heart*

An imperial suite: two to the right
and two to the left, embraced
                      by brazen lungs—

from blue to black
                   the blood
circuits and streams,
aged corridors stiff-frozen closed.

                This heavy tripod,
his despair and fall:

how its black and ruddy flow appals.

3. *The red death*

                  had long
devastated the country, coming
like a thief in the night.
The panes here were a scarlet—
the whole seizure, progress
and termination of the disease
—the incidents of half an hour.

4. *Ceased their evolutions*

Anon there strikes the ebony clock
and the uneasy cessation of all
              things, sunk into silence.

Then a buzz, a murmur, and again
the music swells,

and the dreams live and writhe
to and fro

            until the next lapse
his brow reddened,
and the chords of the heart utterly lost.

5. *In the meantime*

it is folly to grieve, or to think:
with wild courage (and the shame of his
own cowardice), he vows that the next
chiming, extremity in blue, will
produce in him no similar emotion.

6. *The mummer*

The rumor of this presence having spread.
The mask which concealed the visage.
The difficulty detecting the cheat.
The cerements untenanted by any.
The features of the face besprinkled with.
The blood-bedewed. The vesture dabbled.
The same solemn and measured step.

7. *The velvet apartment*

        None dare venture here.
To him whose foot falls
upon the sable carpet, there comes
from the near clock a muffled,
emphatic peal—blood: both
                    avatar and seal.

I cannot countenance the dark
clock's life, arrested, nor

the passing of my hand across his face.

Time and Tide

Outside her window, the canal's slow
waters scum green. Unfathomable,

how it never ceases.
Every day is a bad day—

her stomach lurches, motion sick.
You need to quiet your nerves, the doctor says

and prescribes pills, exposure therapy.
My entire life is exposure,

she says and labors alone
to believe it is the river that moves

and not her. Not her room
that has become passenger coach and she

its rider while all of the world stands
still as she pulls out of the station—no,

not her—slowly at first then
faster and faster until

she's reduced to ghost blur,
to oily whorl. To finger-smear on glass.

Elegy and Aubade

If 5 a.m.'s blue hour sweeps your brow,
if you dip your head over
a mug's ghostly vapours, unable

to sleep again, if you long
for more, if you feel yourself

go under for the eighth time already
today, go under the black wave,
if you long to depart, if you know

you'll never leave and can't
even tell twilight from twilight and

there are those who would wish you
the very worst or, worse,
wish nothing for you at all, if this

is both elegy and aubade, then let
the particular cast of this day's light

flow blue as scilla in spring, and let
the heave of your lungs make
a song of itself. Let it blanket you.

Forgiveness

Another day macerates her bones. On and on, she thinks, though only to herself. She thinks of her children, now grown, of serrated wheels and levers, and then of teeth and jaws, and this produces—inevitably—the image of an enormous, masticating clock. What else?

She is middle-aged now. Gnashing.

The sun rises and she belts her robe snug about her waist. She will tell her husband when he wakes, will confide in him with the same thudding chest that once accompanied the divesting of clothes. She will tease her mind's sash, lift and string it ajar, and let him behold at last her inner-scape. A land of depravities: a creature composed entirely of left feet, a mirror hung from a cliff that can only be viewed from mid-air, her spirit whooshing and rocking a field of phosphorescent pods. And that something that bears her face, that is to say, the one that ripples beneath her mask.

He will nod and fix her the usual cup of coffee. Twenty years. Milk, no sugar.

She knows that he knows. She doesn't need to say it.

The Year I Turned Old

was the year I learned to turn it
all off, mask flat and gray as chert.
Betrayal settled over

my shoulders and chest, a lead-
lined apron, and I accepted
how the heart fails, emergency

room calls, my husband's liquor
cached behind a bucket of sidewalk
chalk. Stubs half-used, left over

from last year. The year
I turned old was the year I learned
to fall numb is not to fall

out of pain. False calm
imposes its own, particular
sentence: the anesthetic's prick,

burning ganglion, the mob
of familiar eyes that will no longer
meet my own. *How could you*

not know? No way to explain
our love—my shame—
like an unset bone

that may never heal quite straight.

The Fall of Manna

after the painting by Fabrizio Boschi (1594-1597)

I do not need to be told
how we are forced to gratitude

through famine and pain.
Forty years of loss: my woman's lot.

I cast my eyes down, clutching
this vacancy like a humble pewter

bowl holds its emptiness,
its doubt. I am a mouth

full of tamarisk, of dust,
faith's word mere silver lichen.

The heart stutters and stops.
Death is a shawl we stretch our limbs

beneath. Sunken ribs, no heart
or lungs to swell and contract,

nothing to break the quiet.
—Sand fans the emptied sky—

How much I would give for relief,
for love restored, for a gift that

comes before it is too late.
Tooth-white, this rain of old age.

How much I desire my hair
to whiten, not with labor, but with

the flowering drift of promise.
To hear manna fall

not in silence but in ash-song—
words woven into hymn,

gentling me like a mother's hand
skims her daughter's head.

To lower my bowl, scoop up
hope and then, greedy, to lift the hem

of my dress to cradle and catch
whatever else I may have missed.

Notes

"A Narrative of the Captivity and Restoration of Mrs.":

The poem titles in this section are derived from the Puritan text, *A Narrative of the Captivity and Restoration of Mrs. Mary Rowlandson.* The epigraph is by Emily Rosko.

Each section of "Impossible Object" is in conversation with works of art that employ a type of optical illusion known as an impossible figure. The first and third reference lithographs by M.C. Escher: "Belvedere" (1958) and "Ascending and Descending" (1960). Section two references "Apolinère Enameled," a 1916 "rectified readymade" by Marcel Duchamp, to which he said he added the "missing" reflection of the back of the girl's head in the mirror above the dresser. This reflection would be as impossible as other items in the room, given the necessary angle for reflections.

The epigraph to "Tableaux Vivants" can be found in the introduction to the 1860 book, *Home Pastimes; or Tableaux Vivants,* by J.H. Head.

Acknowledgements

Thank you to the journals in which versions of the following poems initially appeared, sometimes in different forms and/or under different titles.

Alaska Quarterly Review: "Anger, According to Mrs."

Antioch Review: "The Wedding Processional, as Sung by Mrs."

Black Tongue Review: "Gaslighting"

Cincinnati Review: "The Year I Turned Old" and "Forgiveness" ("Another day macerates her bones.")

Coal Mountain Review: "The Visitation"

Crab Orchard Review: "The Fall of Manna"

FIELD: "The Wedding at Cana" and "Tableaux Vivants"

Gulf Coast: "Tensile"

Memorious: "Time and Tide"

Mudlark: "Three Soliloquies, as Performed by Mrs." (part 1)

Notre Dame Review: "Incarnadine," "Fragments for My Father," and "A Narrative of the Captivity and Restoration of Mrs."

The Southern Review: "Whetstone"

Valparaiso Poetry Review: "Forgiveness" ("Branches toothed and berried…")

Willow Springs: "Three Soliloquies, as Performed by Mrs." (part 3)

Photo by Amanda Crim

Rebecca Dunham is the author of four collections of poetry: *The Miniature Room* (TSUP, 2006), *The Flight Cage* (Tupelo Press, 2010), *Glass Armonica* (Milkweed Editions, 2013), and *Cold Pastoral* (Milkweed Editions, 2017). She has received an NEA Fellowship and was a fellow at the Wisconsin Institute for Creative Writing. Her poems have appeared widely in journals such as *The Antioch Review*, *FIELD*, *The Southern Review*, and others. She is Professor of English at the University of Wisconsin-Milwaukee.

Editor's Choice

2018: Rebecca Dunham
Strike

2017: Todd Fredson
Century Worm

2016: Matthew Minicucci
Small Gods
Mark Irwin
A Passion According to Green

2015: Claire Bateman
Scape
David Blair
Arsonville

2014: Adam LeFevre
A Swindler's Grace
Myronn Hardy
Kingdom
Jennifer K. Sweeney
Little Spells

2013: Judy Halebsky
Tree Line

2012: Cullen Bailey Burns
Slip
Katie Peterson
Permission

2011: David Keplinger
The Most Natural Thing
Mark Irwin
Large White House Speaking

2010: Khaled Mattawa
Tocqueville